Katy's Book of Inspirational Prayers

KATY'S BOOK OF INSPIRATIONAL PRAYERS

Kathleen Copeland

KATY'S BOOK OF INSPIRATIONAL PRAYERS

iUniverse books may be ordered through booksellers or by contacting:

iUniverse
1663 Liberty Drive
Bloomington, IN 47403
www.iuniverse.com
1-800-Authors (1-800-288-4677)

Because of the dynamic nature of the Internet, any web addresses or links contained in this book may have changed since publication and may no longer be valid. The views expressed in this work are solely those of the author and do not necessarily reflect the views of the publisher, and the publisher hereby disclaims any responsibility for them.

Any people depicted in stock imagery provided by Thinkstock are models, and such images are being used for illustrative purposes only. Certain stock imagery © Thinkstock.

ISBN: 978-1-4917-7070-2 (sc)
ISBN: 978-1-4917-7069-6 (e)

Library of Congress Control Number: 2015909971

Print information available on the last page.

iUniverse rev. date: 07/29/2015

I would like to dedicate this book of prayers to my wonderful husband, Marvin Dell Copeland; to my mother, Annie Bell Billups Clifton; to my grandmother, the late Nora Bates Clifton; to my dad, the late Thurman L. Clifton Sr.; and to my brother, Thurman Clifton Jr.

ACKNOWLEDGMENTS

I would like to thank my husband for taking care of me during this difficult time of recovery. From September to November 2014, you never left my side.

To my children, Marcus, Marquita, and Lauren: thanks for all the help.

To my grandchildren, Nyiesha, Keinan, Marquise, and Nyah: Grandma loves you for all you did to keep me comfortable.

To Dr. Geiger: thanks for letting God guide your hands during four hours of surgery.

To my mother-in-law and the Seventh Day Adventist prayer warriors: thanks for all the phone prayers.

To my pastor, Rev. George Waddles: thanks to you and to the Second Baptist Church family for all the prayers, cards, and visits.

To my sisters, Ann and Debbie: thanks for having my back.

To my brothers, James, Jerry, Pastor Larry, David, and Lemar: I love you. Thanks for all the support shown to me and my husband.

To my sisters-in-law: thanks for feeding my husband his vegetarian meals.

To Joyce, my good friend of fifty years: thanks for calling every day to check on me. Love you.

To Darlene, Geri, Edna, Juliette, Mary, Gwen, Darnetta, Jo-Ann, Nikki, Phyllis, Bertha, Anna, Diantha, and Marlene: God puts people in your life for a reason. You are loved so much.

INTRODUCTION

Katy's Book of Inspirational Prayers contains actual prayers that I prayed daily. I have a personal relationship with the Lord that goes back to 1959, and I wanted to share some of God's blessings with others. I believe that if God has blessed you, you need to tell somebody that you asked God to help you and that he did exactly what you asked him to do. Maybe someone will be interested enough to want to get to know the Jesus that you talk about.

When I was at my lowest, living a life of sin, God still blessed me. I still had the sense to pray, even when I was doing wrong and knew I was wrong. In the midst of my mess, God never left me. He showed me my faults, and then he put them in the sea of forgetfulness, never to bring them up again. I made God a promise that I would serve him until the day of my death.

Dear God,

On July 19, 1952, I was a skinny little baby born to Annie and Thurman Clifton. I knew I was special because I was born with complete situs inversus: all my organs are on the side opposite the normal position. My heart is on the right for a reason. I love you, Lord. We live in a small house in Fulton with no indoor plumbing. We have to draw water from the well. Bless us, Father, with a new house.

Dear God,

It's May 1960, and you answered my prayer. I'm eight years old now, and we are moving to a place called Ypsilanti, Michigan. My grandma Nora says the same God she taught me to pray to will be in Michigan also. She said to talk to God every day and tell him what I need.

Dear God,

It's May 1960. I was enrolled in Perry Elementary School. I met two friends, Diantha and Joyce. We live near each other, and we play together every day. I know we will be friends for a very long time. Thank you, God, for putting good people in my life.

Dear God,

My grandmother taught me how to pray to ask you to provide for all of my needs and to work for what I want. Lord, help me to adjust to the ways of Michigan. My life is much faster here than it was in the South. I give thanks to you for moving us safely to Michigan. Please continue to bless my family. In Jesus's name I pray. Amen.

Dear God,

It's November 11, 1961. I joined the Second Baptist Church. My soul feels so good after getting baptized in the name of the Father, the Son, and the Holy Ghost. I'm ready to serve the Lord. I want to be a witness for Christ wherever I go. I will sing praises to you in the angelic choir. I will be a young missionary in the Junior Red Circle. I will be a doorkeeper in your house, Lord, to serve you at all times. Thanks for giving me a humble heart.

Dear God,

I dedicate my life to you. I'm going to move from this place down here on earth to a home not built by man's hands. When you hear me singing my song, I'm trying to get a little closer to my new home that you have prepared for me. I want to walk the streets that are paved with gold. I want to look upon your face. I want to see my father again. In order to do this, I know I will have to live a righteous life. Give me strength to make it in.

Dear God,

I was told that I have an old soul because I pray like my grandmother used to. Thanks for the wisdom and knowledge that you have given me. Continue to bless my life. I'm not perfect, and I make mistakes, but I do ask for forgiveness for all my sins. Thanks for being in my life. I love you, Lord, with all my heart. Thanks for grace and mercy. If I've ever needed you, I need you now. Thanks for putting good people in my life, people who tell me when I am wrong and who help to keep me on the right pathway. I love you, Lord.

Dear God,

I'm your servant, standing at the door, knocking. I'm waiting to hear you say, "Come on in and sup with me, and I will sup with you." Please create in me a clean heart and a renewed spirit so that I can live with you forever. You said in your Word that if you went away, you would come again and receive me unto yourself—that where you are, I may be also. Thank you, God.

Dear God,

You are my Savior, my Prince of Peace, my lily of the valley, my bright and morning star, my *Jehovah Jireh*, my King of Kings. I love to call your name. Your line is never busy, and you are always on time. Bless your holy name. Bless me, Father, and forgive the sins of those who don't know you.

Dear God,

I'm waiting patiently on you. Whatever I do, I ask you for an answer. You said in your Word that those who wait upon the Lord shall renew their strength. They shall mount up on wings like an eagle. They shall run and not get weary. They shall walk and not faint. That's why I am going to wait until I get an answer from you. It may not come when I want it, but it's always on time. You are an on-time God.

Dear God,

I'm in trouble. I need you to hide me with the feathers of your wings. Please let your wings be my shield and buckler. I don't want to be afraid of the terror by day or my enemies by night. I need you to take hold of my hand and lead me on through the storms of life. Sometimes I get weak, and the devil is all around me. I'm trying to resist him, but I need a little help from you. You said to ask and you would give me whatsoever I desire. When I pray and ask in Jesus's name and believe, I receive it in the name of the Father, Son, and Holy Spirit.

Dear God,

Help me to be steadfast, unmovable, unchangeable, always abounding in the work of the Lord. I want to continue to put you first, before anyone or anything in my life. I love you, Lord. I will lift my voice to worship you. In all things, I give thanks.

Dear God,

I'm praying for total healing for my mom, my grandson, and my sisters and brothers, who are fighting diabetes. I'm praying for those I don't know, who are suffering from all kinds of sickness. I'm praying for this world, that we may have peace. I'm praying for all churches, that we may come together and realize that we are all serving the same God. Help us to know that you are the head of all things. No matter what church name we have, you are coming back for that church without a spot or blemish. Thanks, God, for being the head of my life.

Dear God,

I'm your servant, calling on you to help me not to give in to evil but to cleave to that which is good and acceptable, your perfect will. Help me not to conform to this world but to be transformed by the renewing of my mind. Help me to stay strong in my faith and to always acknowledge you.

Dear God,

I want to be a soul winner for you. I want to bring others to Christ by telling them of your goodness and wondrous works. You said to go and teach all nations, baptizing them in your name and teaching them to observe all things that you have commanded us to do, so that you can be with us until the end of the world.

Dear God,

I need a financial blessing. You said that we are to bring all our cares and concerns to you and leave them there. I believe in your Word, and I know if it's your will, I will be blessed. Thanks for giving me a praying spirit.

Dear God,

I'm pressing on the upward way. New heights I'm gaining, each and every day. As long as I live, I know trouble will come, but I will hasten to your throne. I've come too far to turn around now. I love you, God, and I bless your name.

Dear God,

I need your help badly. I can't fly with one wing. Send me another one so I can fly away from here. My heart, my soul, and my mind are heavy. I'm feeling broken. I need to hear a word from you so you can put me back together again.

Dear God,

My soul says yes. I surrender to your will and to your way. I bow down before you, Lord. I truly say yes. I'll do whatever you want me to. Whatever you require of me, I say yes!

Dear God,

It's May 2012. I'm feeling so blessed today. You keep on blessing me, over and over again. Thanks for opening up a window and pouring out on my family a blessing that's too much for us to receive. Thanks from the bottom of my heart. I love you, and I give you all the glory.

Dear God,

I'm living my life here on earth as your child, preparing myself to move from my home down here to my new home that you have prepared for me. In your house, there are many mansions, and the streets are paved with gold. There will be no more crying. Every day will be like Sunday. Thanks for creating in me a clean heart, that I may strive to live for you all the days of my life. And I will join you in the home you made for me.

Dear God,

It's September 27, 2014. I fell, and I need surgery. I'm praying for total recovery—no limping, no more pain, and no back problems. I ask this in Jesus's name. Amen. I'm trusting and believing. If it's your will, it will be done.

Dear God,

I offer prayers for the young women and men who are waiting to be married. I pray that they will seek you first. I know you will pick the best of the best for them. If we choose by ourselves, we sometimes make a mess with all the wrong ingredients. Mixing a worldly person with a godly person will spill over into a half-baked marriage.

Dear God,

Thank you for the opportunity to travel all around the world. You kept me safe, night and day. Your angels watched over me and protected me from hurt, harm, and danger. Thank you, God. No weapons formed against me shall prosper.

Dear God,

It's November 2014. Thanks for watching over me while I was in the hospital. You were there at all times, guiding the surgeon's hand. When I needed you the most, you sent grace and mercy to protect me. Today was not my set and appointed time. Thanks.

Dear God,

Thanks for two beautiful children, Marcus and Marquita. They are my everything. They love you and praise you, just as I do. They have given me four grandchildren, and one great-grandchild is on the way—a little boy. Please put a fence all around them every day. Thank you for letting me make a home for them to grow up in. Thank you for letting me teach them about you and about how to love others as you love us. I give you all the glory and all the praise for helping me raise them and for bringing them to you. Thanks.

Dear God,

I have had some weary days and some hills to climb, but I was faithful to you. Even when I did wrong, you never left me. You said that a saint is just a sinner who has fallen and gotten back up. Thanks for picking me up, turning me around, and placing my feet back on solid ground. You have given me prayer warriors that I can call on anytime, no matter what the problem may be. Darlene, Joyce, Diantha, and Jo-Ann will be there. Corliss, Juliette, Mary, and Gwen will be a prayer away. Thank you, God, that I will always have you.

Dear God,

It's July 3, 2006. Thanks for blessing me with an amazing husband. This man was designed just for me. It took thirty years, but you had to make him just right for me and me for him. You gave me stepchildren, Kim, Lauren, and Marc, and I even got grandchildren from our union: Taylor, Jaylin, Marcus, Jayden, and Imani. Mrs. Jones, a woman I came to love as my mother, introduced us, and we have been married eight years. Thanks for sending me a loving, Christian man.

Dear God,

As I look back over my life, I can truly say that I've been blessed by you. You brought me here from a four-room house with a washing machine on the front porch. We grew all of our vegetables, killed our hogs for meat, made our own soap, and got our eggs from the chicken coop. I know I have been blessed. After coming from a home with an outhouse, I now live in a five-thousand-square-foot home with four and a half bathrooms. Thanks for giving my parents the mind-set to move.

Dear God,

The children in Michigan are mean and evil. Make them disappear. They laugh at the way we talk, and they want to fight. I go home crying every day. Mom says if I come home crying again, she will make me cry harder. From then on, I picked up a brick, and it was on. Sorry, God, for fighting. I forgot that no weapons formed against me shall prosper.

Dear God,

Thanks for watching over me and my family for sixty-two years. My dad and brother are sleeping in heaven, and my aunts and uncles are there also. My grandma and granddad went first. Thank you for keeping me saved and filled with your precious Holy Ghost. You are my rock and my salvation. You are my light in darkness. You are my *Jehovah Jireh*, my provider. Through your Word, I have learned not to lean on my own understanding but to seek you first. Thanks for blessing me with a giving heart that is always ready to help others. If you never bless me again, I still want to say thank you. Your death on the cross for my sins was enough. I love you, Lord, and I will lift my voice to worship you all the days of my life. When it's my set and appointed time to move from this place to my heavenly home, send me two wings so I can fly on up to heaven, sit down at your welcome table, and shake hands with Matthew, Mark, Luke, and John. But most of all, I want to hear you say, "Well done, good and faithful servant. You have been faithful over a few things. Now I will make you ruler over many things. I will give you a crown of life. I have prepared a place for you in my Father's house." I ask these and all blessings in Jesus's name. Amen.

Dear God,

My hope is built on nothing less than Jesus's blood and his righteousness. I pray that I can continue to tell others that you died on the cross so that we may have eternal life with you. God, I pray that I can continue to tell others who don't know you that you healed the sick and raised the dead, that you fed five thousand souls and turned water into wine. Help me to tell others that you took the sting from death. I love you, Lord. Thanks for all your blessings.

Dear God,

Your servant is calling on you. I pray for health and strength today, for there is pain in my body. I know you are the great healer of all pain. Bless those who are sick in hospitals, nursing homes, and their own homes. Forgive me for all my sins. Create in me a clean heart and a renewed spirit so that I may live for you all the days of my life. I ask these prayers in Jesus's name. Amen.

Dear God,

Thank you for waking me this morning in my right mind. Thanks for keeping robbers, fire, death, and sickness from us as we slept during the night. Thanks for my family's health and strength. You have shown us so much favor, and I am so grateful. Father God, thanks for every day that you give my mom here on earth. She's without pain, and I say thank you. Help me to be able to accept your will when you call her home. I pray for wisdom as I continue to study your Word. These and all blessings I ask in the name of Jesus. Amen.

Dear God,

I'm feeling weak, weary, and worn. Help me to stop stressing over things I can't change, but give me the strength to face my problems. Father, I know that if you bring them to me, you will help me to conquer them. I give thanks for all things—the good as well as the bad. Bless my finances, and help me to meet all my needs. Thanks for my health and strength. Bless those who don't know you. Bless the sick and the shut-ins. Bless those in prisons—the ones who are not trying to ask forgiveness for their sins. Thanks for loving us when we don't love ourselves.

Dear God,

I'm giving thanks to you for bringing me, my family, my friends, and my enemies safely into 2015. Thanks for another year. I pray that 2015 will be better for all of us. Thanks for turning on the light in my life. I remember being in darkness, but once you opened my heart to hear your Word saying to come out of darkness into the precious light of God, I never turned back. When I'm in trouble, I call on my Counselor, whose name is Wonderful. When I'm sick, I call on my doctor, whose name is Jesus. I give thanks for being saved, sanctified, and filled with the Holy Ghost.

Dear God,

My heart is so heavy. Today my extended family lost our great-niece to gun violence. Please give us strength to bury such a young woman. Bless the mother and sisters. I pray that they can find comfort in you. Father, put a hedge of protection around my children and grandchildren. Keep them from all hurt, harm, and danger. Bless the sick and shut-ins. Bless those in fighting countries. Keep our president and his family safe. Continue to bless my mom with good health and strength, and let her fight to stay here. I need her to stay here a little while longer, for me as well as for my siblings. In Jesus's name I ask these and all blessings.

Dear God,

I give thanks for all things. I pray that my steps will continue to be ordered by you. Give me the strength to accept your will when it comes to my mom's health. She says she's tired and doesn't want to fight to stay here. I'm grateful that I've had her here for eighty-eight years. Bless the sick and shut-ins all over the world. Please bless my family in a mighty way. Help me to accept the things I cannot change. Bless those who don't want to see us make it. Keep my enemies as my footstool. Forgive me for all my sins. In Jesus's name I pray. Amen.

Dear God,

Today is the day that the Lord has made. I will rejoice and be glad in it, giving thanks for all things. Thanks for waking me up this morning with a reasonable portion of health. Thanks for protecting us while we slept last night. You kept the thieves and robbers away. You kept death, sickness, and fire away from our door, and for that I say thank you. I will forever trust in you and your Word. You said in your Word that those who wait upon the Lord shall renew their strength. They shall mount up on wings like an eagle. They shall run and not get weary. They shall walk and not faint. I will wait patiently on you. These and all prayers I ask in Jesus's name. Amen.

Dear God,

I'm giving thanks for my mom. It's been two years, and she's still here. Doctors gave her six months to live with dialysis, and three months to live without it. She chose not to have it, and by your grace and mercy, she's still here. Thank you, Lord. My prayer is that she will see her ninetieth birthday.

Dear God,

Today is February 8, 1926. A bouncing baby girl was born to Syvilla and Tom Billups. She grew to be a wonderful and beautiful woman, who fell in love and married the love of her life, Thurman Clifton. To this union, eight children were born: five handsome sons and three beautiful daughters.

Annie Billups Clifton was a hardworking woman who decided early on to raise up her children in the church. She told her husband, "I'm going to be a Sunday school teacher, and you will be superintendent of the Sunday school. I'll put the girls in Sunshine Band, Junior Red Circle, youth group, and choir. The boys will be in Boy Scouts, and I will teach the group." Her children grew up to be amazing and responsible adults.

Annie decided to have a little talk with Jesus. She said, "You gave me eight children, and now I'm giving them back to you. Cover them with your love and blood of protection. Create in them a clean heart and a renewed spirit to live for you all the days of their lives. No weapon formed against them shall prosper. If I'm here when it's your time to call and my children's time to answer, take me and let me go and prepare a place for them—that where I am, they shall be."

Now, I lay me down to sleep. I pray to you, Lord, that you will keep my soul. If I should die before you wake me, I pray, Lord, that you will take my soul. This is your servant, Lord. I ask these and all prayers in your name: Jesus, the Christ, the Son of God.

Dear God,

Sweet Jesus, oh how I love your name. I give you all the praise, honor, and glory. Thanks for another day of life. Thanks for keeping me and my family safe. Thanks for a husband I love and who loves me. I give thanks for my mother's health and strength. Lord, help me to continue to show kindness to the less fortunate people with whom I come in contact. I pray for those who don't have shelter or food. Please take care of them and place someone alongside them. These and all prayers I ask in Jesus's name. Amen.

Dear God,

I just want to say thanks for all that you have done for me. I'm not asking for anything. I just want to give thanks for what you have already blessed me with. If you had not died and risen on that third and appointed day, we would not be here to say thank you. No man could have done what you did—only God himself. I'm your servant, standing at the door, knocking and waiting to hear you say, "Come in and sup with me, and I will sup with you in my Father's house." I want to hear you say, "Servant, well done. You have been faithful over a few things, and now I will make you ruler over many things in my Father's house. You have been faithful unto death, and now I will give you a crown of life."

Dear God,

Every knee shall bow, and every tongue must confess that you alone are God. What you did on the cross of Calvary, no man could have done. You hung, bled, and died for me out there on the cross. You stayed in the grave until that third and appointed day, and then you got up for me. Thank you. When I think of your goodness and all that you endured, I can't help but give you glory.

Dear God,

I was glad when they said unto me, "Let us go into the house of the Lord." God, I'm feeling weak and worn. Please give me strength to stand the tests and trials of my life. I pray that I will be able to bless my children and grandchildren with the desires of their hearts. Lord, help me stay true to you and to myself. In Jesus's name. Amen.

Dear God,

I'm giving thanks for another day of life. Thanks for a reasonable amount of health and strength. Thanks for protection as we slept last night. Thanks for keeping Mom safe through the night. Bless those in hospitals, convalescent homes, and prisons, and those who are sick in their own homes. I pray for all seniors. Keep our children safe, Lord. Put a fence all around them, for the devil is busy trying to get them, one by one. I ask your blessing upon my church and upon the pastor as he ministers to us. Father God, I give thanks for all things. Had it not been for your love, I wouldn't be here today. Continue to bless my husband as he works to care for his family. I pray for the bereaved families. Give them the strength they need to bury their loved ones. Forgive me for all my sins. In Jesus's name I pray. Amen.

Dear God,

Our Father, who art in heaven, hallowed be your name. Your kingdom come, your will be done on earth as it is in heaven. Give us this day our daily bread, and feed us with manna from on high. Let us forgive one another and not covet our neighbor's house. Help us to always be ready for reconciliation. Lead us not into temptation, but deliver us from evil. Make our pathway straight. In Jesus's name I pray. Amen.

Dear God,

Help me not to worry about the things of this world but to remember that you know our needs and will bless us according to our needs. First, we must seek your kingdom and your righteousness, and then all other things will be added to us. Help me not to judge others. It's not my job to judge; it's yours. Help me to look for the good in everyone. Thanks for giving good things to those who ask you for them. Father God, help me to continue to study your Word so that I can recognize false pastors who come in lambs' clothing but are inwardly nothing but wolves. These prayers I ask in the name of Jesus. Amen.

Dear God,

I'm your servant, asking you to pick me up after falling. I know a saint is nothing but a sinner who has fallen and gotten back up. The devil is busy, running rampant, trying to find someone to devour. Please keep him away from me. I will resist the devil, and he'd better flee from me. I am your servant and will honor you all the days of my life so that my days may be longer upon this earth. Take my hand and lead me on. I love you, Lord, with all my heart and soul. These prayers I ask in Jesus's name. Amen.

Dear God,

Let the spirit of the living God fall fresh on me. Use me as a vessel to tell others of your coming. Teach me to wait patiently on a word from you and to put you first in everything I do. Things that are done decently and in order will fall into place. Help me to show nothing but love to my enemies. When I'm knocked down, talked about, misused, or abused, let me continue to stand for righteousness.

As I take this walk in the newness of Christ, please keep me humble. Let me tell others that you died on Calvary for all of us and that you are coming back again. Lord, help me to fear no evil, for I know you are with me in all that I do. Thanks for being a lawyer in the courtroom, a doctor in the sickroom, and a friend when I was friendless. Thanks for peace in the midst of a storm. Thanks for unconditional love. In Jesus's name. Amen.

Dear God,

Thanks for giving your only begotten Son to die for us so that we may have eternal life. All we have to do is believe that Jesus died on the cross and that he stayed in the grave for three days before rising on that third morning with all power in his hand. I pray that I will continue my relationship with you. I know I can do all things because you strengthen me. You said in your Word that whoever believes in you shall have everlasting life. In Jesus's name I pray. Amen.

Dear God,

Today someone very dear to us went home to be with you. Give us the strength to accept your calling, even though we are broken. Lift us up, for no one can heal a broken heart except you. Bless the family as they come to grips with their loved one being gone from this life to start a new life in heaven. My prayer is that those who don't know you will get to know you if they want to see their loved ones again. To be absent from the body is to be present with the Lord. I ask these blessings in Jesus's name. Amen.

Dear God,

I give thanks for all things and ask for nothing. Create in me a clean heart and a renewed spirit so that I may live for you all the days of my life. Help me to continue to tell others that I know a man who gave his life one Friday on Calvary—a man named Jesus. He stayed in the grave all day Saturday, and then, early on Sunday morning, he got up from the grave with all power in his hand. Lord, help me to witness to everyone I know, telling them that you died for our sins. In Jesus's name I pray. Amen.

Dear God,

It's a good thing to give thanks unto you, my Father, Most High. You show your loving-kindness in the morning and your faithfulness every night. In all that I do, I give you the honor, the glory, and the praise. I will worship you in all that I do. If it had not been for your mercy, where would I be? I love you, Lord, and I wait on you to come back for your church without spot or blemish. I want to hear you say, "Servant, well done. You have been a faithful doorkeeper, and now you shall wear a crown of glory in my Father's house."